Practicing Silence

Practicing Silence

New and Selected Verses

Bonnie Bowman Thurston

FOREWORD BY BR. DAVID STEINDL-RAST, OSB

PARACLETE PRESS
BREWSTER, MASSACHUSETTS

2014 First printing

Practicing Silence: New and Collected Verses

Copyright © 2014 by Bonnie Thurston

ISBN 978-1-61261-561-5

The Paraclete Press name and logo (dove on cross) are trademarks of Paraclete Press, Inc.

Library of Congress Cataloging-in-Publication Data
Thurston, Bonnie Bowman.
  [Poems. Selections]
Practicing silence : new and selected verses / Bonnie Thurston ; foreword by Br. David Steindl-Rast, OSB.
    pages cm — (Paraclete poetry)
  Summary: «Although the literary form is poetry, this is a book about the spiritual life. Think of it as an armchair visit to a monastery. Focused around monastic themes, it speaks to the spiritual seeker and curious bystander alike by presenting a range of spiritual experiences in accessible language. The poems are grouped according to a monastic logic. A section on visits to monasteries is followed by poems on questions of vocation or spiritual calling that such visits often raise. Then the reader will follow the horarium, or monastic day, and encounter some fruit of lectio divina, the practice of prayerful reading of scripture. The poems on interior prayer will speak to contemplatives in any religious tradition. The collection closes by exploring the experience of anchorites and solitaries. "— Provided by publisher.
  ISBN 978-1-61261-561-5 (paperback)
  1. Spiritual life--Poetry. 2. Monastic and religious life--Poetry.
  3. Hermits—Religious life—Poetry. 4. Contemplation—Poetry. I. Title.
  PS3620.H888P73 2014
  811›.6—dc23   2014016657

10 9 8 7 6 5 4 3 2 1

Published by Paraclete Press
Brewster, Massachusetts
www.paracletepress.com

Printed in the United States of America

Contents

✺ LECTIO DIVINA

Foreword

BR. DAVID STEINDL-RAST, OSB

This book of poems by Bonnie Bowman Thurston stands in an ancient poetic tradition, one that antedates the Protestant Reformation by a thousand years. St. Benedict (AD 480–543 AD), "like a new Moses," his monks said, struck water from the rock of earlier monastic culture; it sprang forth, became a river with many branches, and brought refreshment, healing, and fruitfulness wherever it flowed. Its life-giving water is still flowing strongly today.

John Henry Cardinal Newman spoke of this tradition as the poetical element in the Church and said, "Herein then . . . lies the poetry of St Benedict: in the absence of anxiety and fretfulness, of schemes and scheming, of hopes and fears, of doubts and disappointments."

Silence and inner stillness are the positive signs of this "absence of anxiety," and of the whole list of inner turbulences that follows. But, why? Because stillness is the precondition for listening, and listening in turn is both the essence of Benedictine spirituality and the source of spiritual poetry.

The first word of St. Benedict's Rule for Monks is: "Listen!" All the rest is anticipated and contained in this initial imperative. To listen, every moment, to whatever we encounter, to consider it a word of God, and to respond to that word, that is Benedictine obedience. It is indeed a poetic attitude, since God's Word is not understood as command, instruction, or information, but as a song of praise sung by the Cosmic Christ at the core of every living thing.

Monks who see their vocation in life as joining this chorus of praise, find in it what Meister Eckhart calls "*Gelassenheit*" (defined by Heidegger as "the willingness or ability to let things be as they are," in their uncertainty and mystery). The broad, expansive intellectual and emotional freedom that springs from this attitude has poetic potential. It allows us, as John Keats once put it, to be "in uncertainties, mysteries, doubts, without any irritable reaching after fact and reason." This characterizes Benedictine life at its best. The poems in this book witness to it.

We can also recognize this inner freedom in Bonnie's understanding of her own poetic calling when she admits (in her poem "*The Anchorite – Explains Poetry*"):

> I do it because
> there's nothing else
> I can do.

The ability to squarely face given reality with all its limitations is an essential aspect of genuine inner freedom. It culminates in an awareness of the void inside us. Thomas Merton (another contemporary poet in the Benedictine tradition) calls unflinching confrontation with this emptiness a sacred attitude: "The sacred attitude is one which does not recoil from our own inner emptiness, but rather penetrates it with awe and reverence, and with the awareness of mystery. This is a most important discovery in the interior life." A few lines from *"Through and Beyond"* demonstrate how Bonnie has made this discovery:

> One must be faithful
> to her own, particular
> darkness and doubt,
> walk the way of unknowing,
> live through and beyond
> habituated fears.

Only by approaching darkness and doubt "with awe and reverence," as Merton put it, will we discover the light that shines "in the darkness"—shines not merely into, but *in* the darkness for all those who "will say to the darkness, 'Be my light.'" (Psalm 139:11)

Eyes attuned to this light will see it shine through all created reality, the dark no less than the brilliant. Awe and reverence will characterize the way such eyes look at the world. They will be humble eyes, poetic eyes. Again, according to Cardinal Newman, humility is the prime condition for poetic vision: "The poetical demands, as its primary condition, that we should not put ourselves above the objects in which it resides, but at their feet. We understand them to be vast, immeasurable, impenetrable, inscrutable, mysterious."

When St. Benedict exalts the virtue of humility, he has this down-to-earth attitude in mind. He is aware of the close relationship between the words *humble*, *humus*, *human*—and, not to forget, *humor* that makes us human. In humbly grounding ourselves by kneeling down, we touch the spot where earth becomes transparent to the transcendent. Mary Oliver does so in her well-known poem *"The Summer Day."* While she claims not to know what exactly a prayer is, she does know "how to fall down into the grass, how to kneel in the grass." That's enough and more than enough. Another poet, Rainer Marie Rilke, rejoices that "in a hundred places the world is still enchanted, still retains its pristine freshness, its interplay of pure energy that no one can touch who does not kneel and revere it."

We sense reverence of this kind as we read Bonnie Thurston's poems. The same reverence that made Elizabeth Barrett Browning see "every common bush afire with God" is sensed when Bonnie exclaims:

This whole
remarkable world
is on fire.

Monastic poetry celebrates this fire as the *Lumen Christi*, the light of Christ that shines in our darkness, the way the Paschal candle illuminates the Easter night. The mystic poet Angelus Silesius said of the brilliance of this fire:

God's Radiance is too bright to enter human sight.
The only way to see, is to *become* that light.

Meanwhile, one of the most poetic passages of the Prologue to the Rule of St. Benedict calls it "the light that makes us divine." Ever since I was a novice, it puzzled me that English translations call it simply "the divine light." Had Benedict wanted to say no more than this he had the Latin word *divinum* ready to hand. But he chose the rare word *deificum*. He still belonged to the early Christian tradition of both East and West that did not hesitate to say: "God became human so that we may become God" (St. Irenaeus). Only once, much later, did I meet an official translator of the *Regula Benedicti* and had the opportunity to ask him why he had not translated *deificum lumen* in its obvious sense. To his credit, he frankly admitted, "I simply didn't dare to do so." But then he added, "*Today* I would write 'the light that makes divine.'" I count it a great blessing to have lived long enough to witness theologians beginning to accept what poets knew all along.

Turning the pages of this book, you will find the light that shines in darkness beaming at you as from its author's radiant eyes. Bonnie has spent decades in studying—with both mind and heart—Thomas Merton's writings. Among my most treasured memories are moments of looking into Merton's eyes. In reading some of Bonnie's poems, "Za Zen in Gethsemani Abbey" for instance, I feel again those eyes looking at me. And I remember a poem by Mark Van Doren, with whom Merton studied at Columbia University before he became a monk.

The poem "Once in Kentucky," was the fruit of the first visit the professor paid to his former student at the Abbey of Gethsemani. I would like to close this foreword by quoting it. For, in reading the poems in this book you may well have an experience not unlike Mark Van Doren's. With a smile that "sorrows," Bonnie will taste her joy, then hand it all to you—as much of it as you can carry home with you into a place so different from the monastery. For a moment, you will stand eye to eye with her; and when you have long forgotten the lines of her poems, you will still remember those eyes.

In our fat times, a monk:
I had not thought to see one;
Nor, even with my own poor lean concerns,
Ever to be one.

No. But in Kentucky,
Midway of sweet hills
When housewives swept their porches and March
  light
Lapped windowsills,

He, once my merry friend,
Came to the stone door,
And the only difference in his smiling was,
It sorrowed more.

No change in him, except
His merriment was graver.
As if he knew now where it started from;
And what the flavor.

He tasted it, the joy,
Then gave it all to me:
As much, I mean, as I could carry home
To this country,

To this country whose laughter
Is a fat thing, and dies.
I step across its body and consider,
Still, those eyes.

(*Once in Kentucky* [1] by Mark Van Doren)

Author's Note

While poetry can be a form of prayer, it is not autobiography or history or theology, and poems must stand or fall, succeed or fail, as poems. However, unless one is a strict New Critic or holds a narrow version of the objective theory of art, background information can illuminate a body of written work. And thus the following brief note:

Thomas Merton wrote that "things unknown have a secret influence on the soul." Known things can also have, if not secret, *surprising* influences on the inner life. (And what takes up residence within shapes one's outer life.) This has been the case with monasticism and my soul. I first encountered Christian monasticism nearly forty years ago while writing a doctoral dissertation on Thomas Merton and visiting All Saints Sisters of the Poor Convent (then Episcopalian) in Catonsville, Maryland. I had no idea the influence those two experiences would have on my life. Monastic history, theology, and spirituality, particularly the anchoritic (hermitic or solitary) traditions, got so deeply under my skin that they took up residence in my heart.

I am not a monastic and have no vocation to cenobitic life, knowing only too well the nightmare I would be to a novice mistress and my sisters. But for more than twenty years of widowhood, I have experimented with living more or less as a solitary in the old Celtic mode.[2] Without formal vows, I try in a quiet way to conduct my "ordinary" life monastically, and I can attest that living a monastic spirituality "in the world" is challenging. Various aspects of this experiment have resulted in some of the poems collected here, which are organized according to what I hope is a sort of monastic logic.

Each section is prefaced by a quotation from *The Rule of St. Benedict*,[3] the foundational document of Western monasticism, which sets the tone for and indicates something of the importance of the theme of the section. The selection of poems begins with "Monasteries" because a visit to a monastery is often a person's first introduction to that life and spirituality. Seeing how others choose to live their lives can raise the question of vocation, of one's own calling. The poems in "Vocation" trace a movement toward monastic commitment. The monastic life itself is structured by the *horarium*, the daily schedule of liturgical prayers (Offices) in Choir (the monastic chapel or church). "*Horarium*" gently leads the reader through a monastic day, from Vigils, offered before the sun rises, to Compline, the last Office of the day, which precedes Great Silence and the darkness of night. As part of the rhythm of the monastic day's *ora et labora* (prayer and manual labor), St. Benedict insisted on periods of prayerful reading of Scripture, *lectio divina* (sacred or "divine" reading), represented here by poems that are reflections on scriptural texts. Finally, authentic spiritual life, in whatever context it is lived, is primarily personal, interior, and hidden. This is reflected in "Interior Prayer." The final, brief section of the book explores the expression of monastic life known as the anchoritic, or hermit life.

Although its literary form is poetry, this is a book about the spiritual life. While largely focused on the ancient Christian spiritual traditions of monasticism, these poems, I hope, might speak to both the spiritual seeker and the curious bystander, offering some small light in great darkness, which (*pace* St. John the Evangelist's understanding of God), ultimately, we must come to trust.

Practicing Silence

MONASTERIES

"All guests who present themselves
are to be welcomed as Christ,
for he himself will say: *I was a stranger and you
welcomed me* (Matt 25:35).
Proper honor must be shown *to all,
especially to those who share our faith*
(Gal 6:10) and to pilgrims."

—*Rule of St. Benedict* 53.1–2
(italics in original)

Their Light Shines in Darkness

Out of Egypt
He called His sons.
They migrated
to the islands
at the western
edge of the earth.
Seed of the word,
the classical
and the Christian,
flowered in that
far, foreign soil.
Celtic gardens
preserved its fruit,
illuminated
the waning world
as continents
went slowly dark.

Suppliant

In the monastery
the note said this:
"pick up your tray
at the kitchen door."

Like how many million
suppliants of ages past,
I am to wait at the portal
for Benedict's brethren
to fill my begging bowl.

I do not know exactly
why this makes me smile,
why I am comforted
to be among the indigent
waiting for crumbs to fall
from the monastic table.

But in history's white light
I see myself as I am,
loitering at heaven's back door
empty-handed and hungry,
waiting with the multitudes
for some disciple
to bless, break, and give
God's good bread.

All Saints Convent

In an indifferent world,
Detached from the sands of time,
Your house stands on a rock
And gathers the faceless ones
Around a table
Where the undeserving
Are honored guests.

We come from darkness,
Bring our hungers and thirsts.
We join you, kneel at dawn
Under a single, amber light,
No more strangers,
But sisters in the Silence
Who speaks us all.

Lucubrations

OUR LADY OF THE ANGELS MONASTERY
CROZET, VIRGINIA

Nestled at the base of the Blue Ridge
they begin the day at night,
as earth takes on its contours
pray their way from darkness to light,
allow another self to emerge,
the one healed of its own evil.

They wait in stillness before mystery.
Theirs is the pregnant quietude,
the darkly brilliant expectancy
of Christmas night
when the numinous depths
will deliver a virgin mother.

Their life is useless to everyone but God.
It demonstrates subtraction
is a process of freedom:
the less we own, the more we have.
It encourages increasing receptivity:
the less we grasp, the closer God comes.

Like children by a mountain brook,
they play at the edges of articulation,
amidst an oceanic symphony,
listen for the quiet burble
of a small stream's word,
and, sometimes, hear it.

Monastery of the Holy Spirit

CONYERS, GEORGIA

Just before I arrived
the monks had haircuts.
Heads shaved, robed,
singing in choir,
they looked like a flock
of elderly birds.

The next morning
after Lauds
(I swear this happened),
a pure white dove
landed on a ledge
in the guest house.

Masculine prayers
ascend to the Spirit.
She descends like a dove
on this brood of His love,
like Christ the hen
gathers them in
to the warmth of Her breast,
to the peace of her nest.

Strays

I appear at the kitchen door,
spiritual equivalent
of a wet dog from a storm,
tail tucked, trembling.
You open your lives, this life,
provide prayerful provision,
a vigorous toweling down,
a large bowl of kibbles.
I curl up and sleep safe
on the rug by your heart,
the chapel that warms His,
and so, restored, return
to the weary world rejoicing,
perhaps to provide
a bracing swig
from the fiery word,
perhaps to lead
a lost one home.

VOCATION

"What, dear brothers, is more delightful
than this voice of the Lord calling to us?"

—*Rule of St. Benedict*, prologue, 19

What Do *You* Do?

For far too many years
the teaching, velvet barred
robe, mortarboard, hood,
were a great cover,
an ingenious disguise,
a rubber nose and mustache
attached to fake glasses,
except the charade was
so deadly serious,
legitimate, respected,
gainfully employing words
to hide what matters most:
the empty silence
behind everything else
which infrequently
releases a metaphor
like a single puff of smoke
from a signal fire
just over the brow of a hill,
just at the edge of perception.
Or perhaps it was only
the merest wisp of cloud
returning to wind.
It hardly matters which.
Asked, "what do you do?",
"watch for smoke signals";
"observe evaporation"—
are completely accurate,
utterly unacceptable answers.

Offering

The extroverted, critical rant
of academe did not suit me.
But I knew nothing
else, certainly not that
success at something
doesn't mean one should
give her heart to it.
So I put my head
into the lion's mouth.
But the lion did not close
its saw-toothed jaws.

With my nostrils full
of the stomach stench
of all it had eaten alive,
I withdrew my head
from the dark abyss,
blinked in wonder
at the world's bright beauty,
the green of growing things
to which, as an offering,
a resurrective *fiat*,
I gave my grateful heart.

Through and Beyond

One must be faithful
to her own, particular
darkness and doubt,
walk the way of unknowing,
live through and beyond
habituated fears.

The imprisoned imagination
instinctively knows
chains that bind softly
are still chains
and holding self tightly
poisons the heart.

Many thresholds beckon,
some delightful, some devilish.
The door is always open.
One deep, grateful breath,
one small step forward
has power to change everything.

Forest Dweller

Half a century later
I am tired
of being a householder,
loose the attachment
to its furnishings,
those tawdry trinkets
of the little self,
cast off mooring to place,
but keep a rootedness
in the loam of gratitude
for all that has been.

I will hold no yard sale
lest others carry away
and cling to
trappings of this life.
I will simply
cross the threshold
with only the begging bowl
of an emptied mind,
be a forest dweller,
alone with the universe
and ready.

Veil of Tears

We are born crying
and if fortunate,
they weep when we die.
Between the two we
straddle the abyss,
peer over the edge
of a well of tears,
unfathomable
depths of woundedness
and numb unbelief.

Like Narcissus in
danger of drowning
admiring himself,
we stare down the shaft,
eyes straining to see
the distant mirror,
glimpse our beautiful,
distorted image
in light we obscure.

The invitation
is to shrink the self,
become small enough
for heaven to show
its own hidden face
clearly reflected
from above below
on water's surface,
to hear wafting up

through the fetid stink
and fearsome darkness
faint echoes of song.

Building on Sand

At the outset one is told
to construct the edifice of self
with the best possible material,
great blocks hewn
from the cultural rock.
One builds her tower
to reach toward heaven
until, perhaps halfway
(if she is fortunate),
she understands
this building is illusion,
building on sand.

Then begins the costly
and liberating work
of deconstruction,
breaking the large,
imposing pediment
into small, smooth stones
to skip across life's surface,
send out ripples
toward concentric infinity
before sinking into the depths
where pearls lie
building on sand.

Late Vocation

In the gloaming
when death comes
clearly into view
as the horizon
of life's landscape,
the call is to illumination,
to focus the shining darts
of life's lessons
as a magnifying glass
focuses rays of light.

The task of middle age
is to dispose
of the extraneous,
to focus desire's flickering
until it flames
at the incendiary point
of an undivided heart
and makes of love
a pure, bright blaze
before a falling night.

Dialogues of the Deaf

"The conversations between you and us easily
turn into dialogues of the deaf."

"A Christian Manifesto to the Atheist World"
Madeleine Delbrêl, *We, the Ordinary People of the Streets*[4]

I have reached a stage
of living in a world
of language I don't speak,
language spoken too quickly
to be understood
because its speakers
are in a perpetual hurry
to fill their time
not with the timeless,
but the trivial.

Eternity takes time,
is unconcerned with
bombastic assertions of ego,
the psychologically tawdry,
the spiritually sterile
on which the temporal turns.

We who make ourselves small,
bow to the beautiful
because it is and we can,
listen toward gentler voices
beneath, sometimes within,
the general clamor.

Shunning the expansive self,
its constant chatter that
inflates, conceals, deceives,
we constrict ourselves
into a dense quietude,
a space where speech
is not requisite
because what can be
has been said.
We find it enough.

HORARIUM

". . . nothing is to be preferred to the Work of God."

—*Rule of St. Benedict 43.3*

"The Prophet says: *Seven times a day have I praised you* (Ps 118[119]:164). We will fulfill this sacred number of seven if we satisfy our obligations of service at Lauds, Prime, Terce, Sext, None, Vespers and Compline."

—*Rule of St. Benedict* 16.1–2 (italics in original)

3:00	Rise
3:15	Vigils
6:30	Lauds (Great Silence ends)
7:30	Mass and Terce
	Work I
11:00	End of Work I
11:40	Sext
11:55	Dinner
	Meridian
1:30	None
	Work II
4:00	End of Work II
	Supper
5:30	Vespers and Exposition
7:00	Compline
	Great Silence

Daily Horarium

Even when
staggering sleepily
or stumbling toward
humility and obedience,
the monastic day
is an elaborately
designed dance
in which one knows
one's place.
Prima ballerina
or *corps de ballet*,
all move gracefully,
mirror created order
in the universe,
bring it in
to the body where,
like the Cappadocian Fathers'
round dance of the Trinity,
it spins itself
out relationally
in ever widening
patterns of love,
eternally completing
the unbroken circle.

Offices

Coming to choir
we bow entrance
into mystery:
rippling energy,
opaque, immense,
enduring.
People come and go.
Tragedies erupt.
Emotions disturb.
Joys console.
But this ancient,
placid flow
enfolds them all
like shifting sands
of a great desert
cover all comers,
bare God's stark,
searing beauty.
To chant Psalms
or cower in
blessed interstices
of their silences
is to reflect
light in darkness
until day's sentinels
sound their first
crimson-gold notes
behind earth's
black horizon.

Vigils

Yesterday, brilliant
in the onyx sky,
the morning star
was perfectly aligned
with a baby's thumbnail
slice of moon.

Today, the moon
has waned,
its opalescence
receded into hiddenness
like a woman
behind her veil.

The star still shines,
the treasure given
in impervious darkness,
heaven's vigil lamp,
the finger
pointing the way.

Before Lauds

Great Silence still enfolds
these earliest hours
of the new day,
warm and welcome
as the beds
from which, some alert,
some hazy, we come.

Bound by one brilliant
brooch of light,
day unfolds in layers,
the inky line of hills
with their pink penumbra
shading into the faintest
promise of blue.

The sun eventually
will be ascendant.
But now, in darkness,
the daystar has risen
giving welcome light
to weary wanderers,
hope to a waking world.

Lauds

You are with me,
a gentle embrace
in the aloneness
of the night.
Your Presence
fills my silent room,
lightens my darkness.

Thus with quiet joy
in the morning hour
I go first to You,
beloved in canticle,
Psalm, and Gospel.

The familiar rhythm
of the office
focuses my day,
slowly forms me fearless
as I journey toward night
where You await me.

Paradox

Lauds broke
viscous silence.
The moon hangs
still lustrous
in the ebony west
as crimson tendrils
entwine east's
dark lattice,
thus stabilizing some
precarious balance.
Creation trembles
suspended between
two weighted arms:
the light
in the darkness,
the dayspring
reaching up red
from on high.

Absence and Emptiness

At the heart of a monastery
is the fruitful emptiness
of cloister's garth garden;
the emptiness in the belly
that makes the guts
gurgle through Sext;
the emptiness in the bed,
absence of person
on whom to lavish love,
give and receive
the gifts of body.

These and other absences
clarify and create space,
invite deeper *kenosis*,
teach the darkest voids,
life's blackest holes,
are castles for the King
Who emptied Himself.
At the heart of absence
is fullness of life,
awareness of the prayer
that is always within.

Monk's Prayer

At the monastic center
is always a cloister,
an orchestrated emptiness,
a place of light,
a fountain to feed
the heart's garden.

Give me this life:
a center empty
of all but light,
the stillness of Eden
before fruit was plucked,
my heart a spring
of living water.

Plainchant

Something about chanting
the Psalms settles the heart.

Maybe it's the stepping
into an ancient stream:
quavers, semi-quavers
ascending and falling,
unexpected patterns
old as their first singers.

Perhaps a notation
of squares strung on needles
tames wildest emotions:
hatred and smashing heads,
humility and trust,
crazed, exuberant love.

Perhaps in ego's lapse,
as music and Psalter
collapse history's, time's
old, disparate voices
in one melodic line,
all is rendered peaceful.

Something about chanting
the Psalms settles the heart
which, indeed, is restless
until it rests in praise
of the Joy Who made it
and laughs to receive it.

Untitled

Chanted liturgy of the hours
has its own, peculiar beauty,
but I like chapel best
when peopled by knee bent,
lips closed, hearts open
and beating with the same life,
when no sound disturbs
palpably numinous air,
fitting place into which
to drop a Word.

Between Vespers and Compline

The sun bleeds evening
as day dies red
behind purple hills.
The last half hour
is the sweetest,
when between
Vespers and Compline
the house is silent
for love not rule,
when precious minutes
are squandered
like Mary's precious nard
reading, thinking,
gathering wool,
scratching the cat,
loving You profligately,
in our own time,
in our own way,
by offering the gift
of these last rites.

Vigil Light

A bee-made candle
flickers quietly,
barely light in darkness.

In a red blaze
the electric sign
shouts, "EXIT."

It is like this:
we manufacture all manner
of artificial things,

the brighter, the shinier,
more tawdry, the better
to distract us,

to point the way to exits
which are no exits
but opaque, endless mazes,

distract us from realities
dwelling in murky places
where no voice disturbs the air,

but where, if you linger
and listen, you might hear
the original Voice.

Bee-made light is silent,
emits no electric buzz,
but is sweet to the taste.

Psychic Horarium

How long night is.
How quickly day comes.

After Vigils, *lectio* dark
under full, bright moon.
How long night is.

After Lauds, eastern horizon
bright below murky heaven.
How quickly day comes.

After Vespers, darkness
stalks the vermillion west.
How long night is.

Compline's cry:
How long night is!
Daystar, quickly come!

Compline

Salve, Regina:
Crown of the day,
our Lady's crown,
adult version of
"Now I lay me
down to sleep."
There *are* monsters
under beds, in closets,
prowling, roaring—
terrors, dangers, evil.
We need defenders
against darkness.

And so we close
the day with singing,
abiding in the shelter
of the Most High,
our help in His Name.
But we entrust ourselves
to the eternal Mother,
ever watchful,
always listening,
continual carrier
of light in darkness,
clemens, pia, dulcis.

Great Silence

It is Islam's
laylat al-qadar,
the mysterious night
when heaven opens,
angels descend,
all restlessness stilled,
nature bends in adoration.

The bridegroom
of the Lord's parable
comes at midnight.
He is always near,
always returning,
but never more so
than at dawn's
faintest whisper
when the world hangs
between the passing
and the coming to be.

LECTIO DIVINA

"Idleness is the enemy of the soul. Therefore, the brothers should have specified periods for manual labor as well as for prayerful reading."
—*Rule of St. Benedict* 48.1

Chapter 4. The Tools for Good Works.
"Listen readily to holy reading, and devote yourself often to prayer."
—*Rule of St. Benedict* 4.55–56

". . . the Lord waits for us daily to translate into action, as we should, his holy teachings."
—*Rule of St. Benedict*, prologue, 35

The Sixth Day
—Genesis 1:26–28, 31

No one else can teach you
to read the book of your body.
You must learn its language—
its little, grunting inarticulacies,
its unutterable stillness,
its symphonic movements—
in your own way and time.

The wisdom of the flesh
is deep as earth's dust,
high as heaven's animating wind.
Clay feet tie us to the ground,
but we sail on the sea of the senses,
and our hearts beat
the rhythm of the stars.

No one else can teach you
to read the book of your body,
but you must learn its language.
Trust it speaks truth
and soar on the strength of your scars.
Trust it speaks truth
and wear your wounds as wings.

Sarah
—GENESIS 11:30

I was promised blossoms green and blue.
Though sere and yellow, draw me close today.
My dry and drifting leaves still, hopeful pray
For fluid of the tree from which they grew.
Hold me, and this last summer spangled hue,
My saffron shrouded mourning coat allay
With harvest-haven lingering in the hay.
This palest shade becomes no woman true.
O glean me morning's promised cup of dew.
Plunge deep within my thirsting, empty clay
And pierce the darkness with life's virile ray.
Take me, dust and death, make me fertile, new.

Abram at Haran
— Genesis 12:1

He was seventy-five years old
and God's first word to him
was "Go."

I think of Abram
when my plans go awry,
when happenstance

pries my fingers loose
from the grasping illusion
of control over life.

"Go," God said to Abram,
giving no address,
disclosing no destination.

Taking an unruly family,
trusting God to show the way,
Abram went.

On that wild journey
he, too, had fingers pried loose,
heard Sarai laugh, learned

the blessing comes
in the going
and the letting go.

Peniel

—GENESIS 32:30

by the river Jabbok

You send us
incendiary persons,
shining presences,
who reflect and refract
Your glory.

Radiant like the sun,
in their spiritual combustion
we glimpse
our own light
in a mirror darkly.

Oh surfeit of light!
Hide us in the secret
of Your face
lest illumination
blind us.

The Chosen People
—Exodus 14

Tied to our wells,
we drank deeply,
were coddled,
cared for,
then prodded
from our comfortable slavery
to a land of learning.

Crossing that chasm,
we discovered
deserts of doubt.
No land of milk and honey
on that withered way.

But beyond
mountains of mind
waited sea salvation.
We arose
from parted waters,
and we journey
toward the sun.

Moses

—EXODUS 17:1–7

arid world
weed littered garden
empty husks
one spark
smolders

thirst
swollen-throated
cotton-mouthed
mind-writhing
thirst

beat the rod
against the rock
no water
no water
no water

wither
arid world
broken stalk
hollow pod
lifeless rattle

beat the rod
against the rock
one spark
one flame
burning bushes

here I am
thirsting speechless
put words
in my mouth
water

Rahab's House
—JOSHUA 2:1–21

A crimson thread
hangs in the window
of the woman's house
who took the risk
and protected strangers.

Now, one tiny thread
protects her household,
the thread of trust
that strangers are trustworthy,
that enemies are friends.

Some say she is no better
than she ought to be.
But she is better than most,
and I want to live
in a house like hers.

Jonah

The Word of the Lord came to him,
and he fled it,
as if there were a godless place.
Whither could he go to be
free of God's presence or plan?

Down in the ship's hold, Jonah slept
as the storm grew more tempestuous,
as the sailors threw their cargo
into the deep's ravening mouth.
They woke him to ask,
"Where do you come from?"

If God Who made heaven and earth
is your native country
you can't choose to expatriate.
God dwells in the depths
and at the farthest limits of the sea.

Even when thrown over the side,
cast off like bilge or ballast,
Jonah was swallowed
by the big fish of God's providence;
belched right back into the midst
of God's plans for the Ninevites.

Job

You live in unremitting darkness,
surrounded by an unbearable silence
with which your friends cannot cope.
They fill the air with worthless words,
ugly flies buzzing around your sores.

Your howl of pain, moans in the night,
attempt to shatter the stillness
of divine and distant implacability.
Your cries are sacred songs,
humanity's common lament.

With no more reasonableness
than the cause of your agony,
the eyelids of the morning blink,
give a transitory glimmer
of the wildness behind all suffering.

You glimpse One whose ways are not ours,
Who, blasted by our whys, changes the subject.
For all this unearned, unredeemed pain,
you are recompensed with only the Is-ness of God,
barely enough, but light to wrestle on.

"God has set eternity in human hearts . . ."
—ECCLESIASTES 3:11

Living is a matter of limitation
most of it to do with temporality.
At the outset eternity is sown
deep in the soil of the soul,
planned and planted source
of our rest and restlessness.

Life beckons beyond chronology,
summons with siren call:
"Come to me; I will give you rest."
Leaving time, we enter I AM,
the eternal present tense
of death, liberating plunge
into the long ago planted.

Godmaking

"Then shall the eyes of the blind be opened"
—ISAIAH 35:5

In India, godmaking
is an ancient, sacred trade
conducted with skill and faith.

Between 4:00 and 6:00 AM
when no sound disturbs the light,
the deity incarnates.

The idol is brought to life
when its eyes are created,
opened with golden chisel.

God's presence is always
chipped open by the faithful,
blind belief of devotees.

"Lord, let our eyes be opened"
is a wild, audacious prayer,
for seeing births God within

makes beggars rise and follow
their Master's dusty journey
to Jerusalem and death,

that final chipping away:
ego's cloudy cataract
from sight's truth, fullness, source.

Isaiah 49:25; 54:1–3

Physical generativity past,
the spiritual flourishes,
interior potency predominates,
brings to belated birth
a late life Renaissance
of who we yearn to be.

The God of Sarai, Hagar
mysteriously becomes
the Green Man gone womanish
with vaginal effluvia of vines
lush, fragrant, fecund
with all that feeds,
verdant God trailing tendrils
not to entangle but liberate
freedom already possessed
but often unrecognized.

God is *rehem, beit al rehm*,[5]
merciful source of nourishment,
compassion in Whom we grow,
from Whom we go.
God has always been womb
Who, with a rending shudder,
pushes us further into life.

Isaiah 55:8

God's inexorable predilection
is for all that is small,
broken, and set aside.

Not to the firstborn blessing,
but to the brother far away
tending the father's sheep.

Not to the comely offspring,
but to the old, barren wife
a son to beget nations.

God counts hairs on the heads
of the neglected, naked, and poor
and dances with the sparrows.

God pitched a tent among outcasts,
arrayed in sackcloth and ashes,
weeps with widows and orphans.

Behold on the cross
the Cosmic King
whose ways are not ours.

The Mat
—Mark 2:1–12

Down I went
through a hole in the roof,
stomach churning with fear of falling
into some worse calamity
than wasted legs and years.

"Take your mat, and go home."

O, bitter charge! Not abandon
the symbol of servitude,
but bear the reminder
of a wounded past,
and not to some new place,
but home where I am known
as broken beggar.

Healed and free,
He sends me back
to renew those whom,
like the mat,
I would rather leave behind.

Well Water

"Jesus, tired out by his journey, was sitting by
the well." —JOHN 4:6

"The water that I will give will become . . .
a spring of water gushing up to eternal life."
—JOHN 4:14

Endowed with sacred
character, wells span
three cosmic orders:
water, earth, and air.
Their water is held
by earth, then given
to creatures of air.

Well water bubbles
from hidden places.
It comes from within
the bosom of earth
as one element
offers its essence,
its self, to the rest.

Quiescent and clear,
the living water
settles deep within,
awaiting its time
of rising to light,
of being consumed,
giving life for life.

Feeding Miracle
—JOHN 6:1–15

Philip saw only
the size of the need
that six months' salary
would not feed.

Andrew saw only
insufficient provision,
a small boy's lunch:
five loaves, two fish—
so little for so many.

Jesus saw us,
consumed by hungers,
ravished by appetites,
malnourished in every way.

"Feast on the Word
made flesh," He said.
"Drink my wine
and eat my bread.
I am more than enough."

"But gather up what is left
of my broken fragments.
You will need them for the journey.
They will feed you on the way."

The Stone
—MARK 16:3–4

The Myrrhbearers came
(with what fear and trembling?)
trudging along in darkness
worrying about
the stone.

Everybody worries about
the stone,
that great impediment
between us
and what we seek,

that great burden
we carry
like Sisyphus
laboring
up and down the hill.

The sun rose.
The women looked up.
The stone,
which was very large,
had been removed.

No wonder they ran
to tell Cephas.
Somebody should tell Sisyphus:
"Put it down, man,
and dance on it."

Thanksgiving for St. Thomas

— JOHN 20:24–29

Thomas reached out
to Christ's wounds,
put man's flesh
in God's dark places,
felt his own darkness
and found light.

We, too, left You in the tomb,
have closed ourselves
to open promises.
Those dark, dry days
have been for us death
and bring about birth.

Blind and alone
we enter pain and thirst,
find in that desert,
in that night of choice,
our own, awful beauty.
We pass through that side.

In the darkness that bears
this dawning day,
we reach into Your wounds
and know our own.
By this touch You
make our hands Yours.

Precious Rocks

"I will give a white stone, and on the white stone
is written a new name that no one knows except
the one who receives it."
—REVELATION 2:17

Perhaps this is why
I have always been
a collector of stones,
lined dusty window sills
of home, retreat house,
vacation cabin
with small impediments
of meandering journeys:

a tiny, purple chip
from Sinai's height;

Wyoming soapstone
smeared with copper ore;

deceptively flecked schist
full of fool's gold;

once, in Virginia,
where rock is red
with ferrous oxide,
a three-inch obelisk
of gray granite
fused to milk quartz;

Iona's green marble,
the crimson pebbles
of its martyr's beach;
(my perennial favorite)
a water-worn smooth
white palm-sized stone.

The hand luggage
of my travels
is heavy with them,
the basement littered
with petrified souvenirs
from forgotten places.

Reader, do not chuckle
in bemused indulgence.
"Stony the road I trod."
On life's rocky road,
it is serious business,
to search the hard,
animate beauty of stone
for one's own hidden
and secret name.

INTERIOR PRAYER

Chapter 4. The Tools for Good Works.
". . . devote yourself often to prayer."
—*Rule of St. Benedict* 4.56

"We must know that God regards our purity of
heart and tears of compunction, not our many
words. Prayer should therefore be short and
pure, unless perhaps it is prolonged under the
inspiration of divine grace."
—*Rule of St. Benedict* 20.3–4

". . . we shall through patience share in the
sufferings of Christ that we may deserve also to
share in his kingdom."
—*Rule of St. Benedict,* prologue, 50

Prayer

Prayer is not
scrabbling together
a few paltry words,
flinging them like stones
at the windows
of ineffability.

It is *Gelassenheit*,
letting go,
being carried on a current
toward a vast ocean,
deep beyond imagining;

sitting silently,
gaze firmly fixed
on one golden,
inscrutable face,
waiting
with the patience of love;

pouring out life,
that alabaster vial
of costly ointment,
at the feet of One
Who washes others
with His tears.

Prayer is
asking nothing,
desiring nothing
but this,
only this.

Za Zen in Gethsemani Abbey

Far away
at the other end
of the nave,
the red eye of God
never blinks or closes
by the cave
where Christ reposes,
waits
to be lifted up
and consumed.

In the choir
the rhythm of eternity
beats itself out
in psalm and song.
Into empty space
the Hours drop
illuminated words
like glittering jewels,
treasures for the coffers
of the heart.

I sit in the balcony
beneath azure windows
contracting my self
into the deep recesses
of my body,
drawing myself in,
letting myself go.

I remove ego's clothing,
await the fiery embrace
of luminous stillness,
inhabited emptiness,
wait
to be lifted up
and consumed.

School of the Heart

The prison doors
of preference and pride
must be opened
by humility's patient hand.
The relentless grinding
of the intellect
must be stilled,
coaxed down
into the quietness
of the waiting heart
where it can learn
in a school
like one sees
in mission photographs
from third-world countries,
walls open to the world,
roof perhaps permeable,
impoverished children
intensely eager to learn
the waiting teacher's
lesson of limitless love.

A Burning Deep Within

A burning deep within—
like a mysterious light
glimpsed far deeper in the woods
than you have dared to walk.
A beckoning, "come home":
home to your uniqueness;
home to the home
this world cannot offer,
home to the place you belong,
to that which you love.

To go there you must
develop *apatheia*,
the discipline of detachment
from all that is trivial,
that fragments or scatters,
develop a unifying heart
that gathers like a glass
refracting rays of light
from the source
of the burning deep within.

Darkness at the Edges

Though my inner life
is lived largely in shadow,
You are astounding brilliance,
pulsating, white hot light
magnetic, terrifying,
the comforting challenge
at the core of everything.

Like an unformed thought,
I glimpse in peripheral vision,
darkness at the edges,
a profound emptiness
falling away into eternity.

Is this the hidden shoal
on which the ship founders?
The temptation to leap
from Temple's tower?
The soul's cellar steps
down which one tumbles
like a dervish of despair?

What inhabits darkness?
Is this John of the Cross territory?
Apollinaire's liberating leap?
Give me the blind man's eyes
after he was touched.

Praying into Darkness

". . . what lights our darkness bears a terrible cost."
—JANE HIRSHFIELD, *Nine Gates*[6]

"Lighten our darkness
we beseech Thee, O Lord."
We murmur evening prayer
as darkness prowls
beneath the kitchen window
where, within, hearth fire frightens
"perils and dangers of the night."

Consider the courage
it takes to seek out
wood for the fire,
coal for the stove.
Consider the cost
of darkness breaking,
of light bringing.

Remember Prometheus, fire bringer,
vultures pecking at his liver.
Remember Jesus, light bringer,
nailed to creation's candle,
mockers snarling and scrabbling
beneath him in bloody dust.
Both prayed into darkness.

Inside Out

On the face of it
all appears well,
but mostly wounds
are deep beyond reckoning.
As in surgery
the surface heals,
but in subcutaneous depths
resides an awful, jagged maw
into which one
must eventually walk,
sit down, wait for what
only waiting accomplishes:
victory over restlessness
conquering the urge to control;
acceptance of utter helplessness
inviting help's arrival.
We are all healed
in passive voice
and from the inside out.

Remember I Am Fragile

I am the brittle reed,
the sputtering wick
flickering in the dark,
ravening maw
of this era's biliary beast.
You took the scales
from the eyes of my heart,
removed my soul's filters,
left me utterly
defenseless, prey to

its random physical,
ubiquitous moral deformity;
its befouled diminishment
of the blessed world
we barely, badly steward;
its arachnoid complexity,
evil's intractable webs
knowingly or stupidly spun
but inevitably entangling
Your innocent little ones.

Creator by Word,
Clother of lilies,
Sustainer of sparrows,
remember I am fragile,
easily snapped or snuffed
by the merest movement
of Your mighty wind.

Come to me gently.
Give me the quiet
courage of hope.

Genesis Within

I live in hope
of genesis within,
that God hovers
over the deeps
of internal chaos,
anxious to order,
fill vast aridity
with the juice
of flora and fauna.

I have learned
to still the body,
silence the mind,
to wait in obscurity
for any small radiance,
listen with every cell
for any faint echo
of "Let there be light."

The void of expectancy
is a potent place:
pure possibility.
Here, I yearn to learn
the art of birth,
and rebirth,
trust the darkness
does not come down
this far.

De profundis: *Interior Prayer*

When the tempest is stilled,
the water becalmed,
what is reflected
is not always the heavens.

Bent, twisted creatures
demons from the deep
born in darkness,
blind from birth,
devilish dervishes,
surface unbidden,
smash the shallow placidity
of partial openness,
reveal how imperfectly healed
are the deepest wounds.

Janus-faced companions,
they remind us
by their clamor
that, regardless of cost,
gradually, continually,
true stillness always
tends toward light,
toward what their world
is dying to know.

Acquiescence

Once again the darkness
has fallen suddenly.
Without warning the miasma
descends and engulfs.
I must navigate
another psychic night
without buoy, bell, lighthouse.

This odd, choppy journey
seems charted for me,
the tacking route
to whatever sanctity
has been appointed.
It has become a familiar,
known, despised, accepted.

Resistance is fruitless,
casts me more adrift
than graceful submission.
This is who I am,
discover in surrender
the tentative light
of a distant star.

Supplication

Give me courage:

To put my head
on a stone
and not flinch
when angels come
down the ladder;

When summoned
to run
across the lake;

When commanded
to cast my empty net
one more time;

To believe
everybody can feast
on five loaves
and two fish.

Of all the evils
the thief devised
deliver me
from the evil
of resisting life,
refusing the abundance
that is everywhere,
in everything,
even death.

"Be Thou My Vision"

We are shaped
by what we desire.
We become
what we behold.

That being so,
enlarge my vision,
make it wide and clear.
Let me see it all:
princes and paupers,
palaces and shantytowns,
great canvases
and graffiti on a gritty wall,
the stately, the scarred,
the lovely, the leper.
May nothing human
be foreign to me.
Enlarge my heart
to embrace it all.

Strengthen me to bear
such hospitality.
But let my desire
be only for You.

Fiery Impulse

There is a fiery impulse
at the heart of prayer,
not saying prayers,
but primal prayer,
the self's radical
turning toward God
in Whose incendiary gaze
ego's dross is consumed.

The essence left
after the conflagration
wears only the garb of light,
a radiance that passes
from soul to soul.
Glimpsed, not taught,
it illuminates a dark world
with a searing love
that beckons, burns,
ignites a fiery impulse.

It Must Be Prayer

It must be prayer,
drinking in this greenness,
absorbing patterns of wind on water,
walking up the mountain in silent spring,
following the pattern of old roads
that tie my solitude to pioneers
or perhaps first peoples.

Being part of stillness
must be prayer,
as much as the black snake
shedding an old skin,
as much as the indigo bunting,
a blue bead warding off evil,
or the fox, furtive at field's edge.

ANCHORITES,
HERMITS,
SOLITARIES

". . . the anchorites or hermits . . .
have come through the test of living in
a monastery for a long time, and have passed
beyond the first fervor of monastic life.
Thanks to the help and guidance of many,
they are now trained to fight against the devil.
They have built up their strength and go from
the battle line in the ranks of their brothers to
the single combat of the desert."

—Rule of St. Benedict 1.3–5

Solitude

Solitude is not a place, but a way
that questions the cultural package,
pushes away its Pandora's box
of expansion and acquisition
for a certain psychic contraction,
a displacement of self from center,
the knowledge that giving is love.

It cultivates stillness of heart,
seldom speaks wantonly,
bears its own suffering silently.
It receives rather than imposes,
defers rather than asserts,
knows how little is required,
lives richly on next to nothing.

It does not encroach on creation
which responds with myriad delights.
Solitude is sentinel of authenticity,
of the bliss of living alone together.
The solitary sows secret seeds
of a public possibility
that scares the dead to death.

The Anchorite
A SEQUENCE

EXPLAINS SOLITUDE

Living alone
is not a luxury,
but Babylon's furnace,
fierce, refining,
uncushioned.
Unlike Daniel's
three young men,
I come singed,
smelling of smoke.
It is the price
of walking
with the Fourth.

OFFERS A DISCLAIMER

It is not my job
to hold the universe
together,
to solve the past,
to plan the future,
only to be here,
awake.

VISITS A GREAT CATHEDRAL

We do not live our lives
at the High Altar
but in side chapels
of quietude where
what is really present
goes on out of sight
of the nave's big events,
where candlelight flickers
only in peripheral vision.

RISES EARLY

We must rise early.
How else can we see
the sky full of stars,
but low on the horizon,
as if bending
to kiss earth's darkness,
presage dawn's embrace,
provident daily reminder
we are not forgotten?

GIVES THANKS

I thank you
that the day is quiet,
the sun is bright,
that awareness of you
dances in consciousness
like autumn leaves
against the blue sky.
It is a happiness
to need only this much
of your infinite variety,
to love your dying world,
to know love undying.

PRAISES BIRDS

It was a cold night.
A sizeable community
of slate-colored juncos,
charcoal gray coats
bobbing over white bellies,
pick in the frosty grass
where carefully kept
crumbs from the bread board
were flung with abandon.
Perhaps only in this
am I like unto God:
I know them worth
infinitely more than
two for a penny.

AWAITS SPRING

Just when spring
should arrive full of sap,
an Arctic Clipper
rattles through
dropping, once again,
winter's lumpy eiderdown.
Icicles form on gutters,
silvery, arthritic fingers
pointing accusingly
at frozen ground.
Sun on hoarfrost
makes everything glisten.
There is a crisp sound
of ice falling from trees,
the drip, drip, drip of winter's
witch fingers melting,
enlivening waiting earth.

ANTICIPATES EASTER

When the culture
has gone mad
as a March Hare,
the steady sanity
of quiet people
who want to live
alone with God
appears crazy as crocus
poking up through snow,
Lenten purple,
but promising Easter.

EXPLAINS POETRY

I do it because
there's nothing else
I can do.
I was made for
long listening,
solitary watching,
the almost inaudible
Word.

DELIVERS AN IMPERATIVE

In the midst
of the shouting
and squalor
an exquisite lotus
silently unfolds
petal by
intricate petal.
Attend to it.
This whole
remarkable world
is on fire.

Hermit Lessons

A Sequence

For my Brothers at Our Lady of Gethsemani Abbey, Trappist, Kentucky

I.

Taking little with them
but horror
at a world gone mad,
a vast, consuming
hunger for God,
they flee to deserts,
seek quiet places
to be still and know,
lonely, fecund places
where the heart can grow.

But sanctity is magnetic.
Even society's rusty dregs
are drawn to it.
Others come to taste and see.
Love requires
the hungry be fed.
A hermit learns
the way to keep peace
is to give away
even the desire for it.

II.

"Keep to your cell;
it will teach you everything."
Eremitical wisdom of the ages
trades far horizons
for narrower confines.

In a world of perpetual motion
a vow of stability,
to stay put, to be still,
is being walled
in an anchor-hold.

Search down instead of out.
Find within
foolishness, falseness,
lust, avarice, violence—
all you sought to flee.

Find God.
Learn this:
You are never
less alone
than when alone.

III.

After the terrors of the desert—
the hunger and thirst,
the visions and delusions,
the privations and deprivations,
the great and small renunciations
that chip away self's dark wall
until the soul shines through—
after all that, what?

More of the same.

IV.

A pragmatic question:
"What do they do
for a living?"

Answer:
Nothing very useful:
grow a few scrawny vegetables,
weave a misshapen basket,
write poetry,
talk to the birds.

Their real job
is to spin straw
into gold.

V.

An incredulous question:
"Why do they do it?"

Answer:
To throw off
the burden of a world
that asks too much
and offers too little:

to unwrap
God's greatest gift:
the liberty
to grope
toward freedom.

V.

The ultimate lesson?
Live simply.
Simply live.
Rise from the dead.

Little Rule for a Minor Hermitage

Greet the day with thanks
for safety through the night.
Rekindle and nurture this hearth's fire.
Care for life on this bit of land.
Work; pray; rest.
Avoid judgment.
Do no harm.
Think about what matters.
Attend to the body.
Welcome guest and stranger.
Take what comes with gratitude.
Give what is needed with gladness.
Greet nights with courage.
Review the day for small joys
overlooked in living it.
Then, trust the darkness.

Notes

1 Mark Van Doren, *The Autobiography of Mark Van Doren* (New York: Harcourt Brace, 1958), 331-32. Reprinted with the kind permission of Charles Van Doren.

2 For more on this see my contribution "*Soli Deo Placere Desiderans*," in *A Monastic Vision for the 21st Century*, ed. Patrick Hart, OCSO, Monastic Wisdom 8 (Kalamazoo, MI: Cistercian Publications, 2006).

3 All quotations from Benedict's Rule are taken from Timothy Fry, OSB, ed., *The Rule of St. Benedict* (Collegeville, MN: Liturgical Press, 1981). I am grateful to Liturgical Press for permission to use quotations from this edition of the Rule.

4 Madeleine Delbrêl, *We, the Ordinary People of the Streets* (Grand Rapids, MI: Eerdmans, 2000).

5 The Semitic root of "compassion" or "mercy" is "womb": *rehem* (Hebrew), *beit al rhem* (Arabic, literally "house of compassion").

6 Jane Hirshfield, *Nine Gates: Entering the Mind of Poetry* (NY: HarperCollins, 1998).

Thanksgivings

Several of the poems in this volume have appeared previously. I am grateful to *America Magazine, Anglican Theological Review, The Awakenings Review, The Merton Journal* (UK), *The Merton Seasonal* (USA), *Monastic Inter-Religious Dialogue Bulletin, Monkscript, National Catholic Reporter, The Panorama, Presence, Review for Religious,* and *Spirituality* (Ireland) for permission to include material they first published. The poem "All Saints Convent" first appeared in *A Monastic Vision for the 21st Century: Where Do We Go From Here?*, ed. Patrick Hart, (Kalamazoo, MI: Cistercian Publications, 2006), published by Liturgical Press. The following presses have also graciously allowed use of poems that appeared in their books: Cinnamon Press (Wales); Darton, Longman & Todd (U.K.); Fons Vitae (Louisville, KY); and especially Three Peaks Press (Wales), which holds a special place in my heart for having published my first two small collections of verse. If I have neglected a periodical or press, it is certainly an unintended oversight, and I ask forgiveness and the opportunity to add those names to any future edition of this work.

Many years ago All Saints Sisters of the Poor (Catonsville, MD), and more recently two communities of monastic women, the Society of the Sacred Cross, Tymawr Convent (Wales) and Our Lady of the Angels, a Cistercian monastery near Crozet, VA, have offered generous hospitality and exerted a now not-so-secret influence on my soul. These sisters will, I expect, recognize (I hope without horror) a number of things in these poems. I hope they know how profoundly grateful I am for their presence and influence in my life.

Although New Directions didn't accept an earlier version of this manuscript, I was greatly encouraged by their editor, Barbara Epler, who took the time to read it. I was completely delighted when Paraclete Press accepted the manuscript and owe Jon Sweeney a great debt of gratitude both for his confidence in this work and his subsequent judicious editing of the manuscript, which Paraclete Press's production team has brought to the lovely reality you hold in your hand. Special thanks to Robert Edmonson for his care with the manuscript and patience with its author.

Many thanks to the trusted and cherished friends who read first drafts of my work, thus giving me confidence to launch some of them publicly: Ruth Bidgood, Stephanie and James Coutts, Esther de Waal, Cheryl and Marc Harshman, Charl and David Kappel, M. Marion Rissetto, ocso, and Jane Rotch.

That Br. David Steindl-Rast provided the foreword for this collection is a source of deep joy for me. He has been a friend since the 1970s, a faithful companion and a profound influence in my life's journey. I am more grateful than he may know. Vielen dank, lieber Bruder.

I hope something of the mystery and spiritual depth of monasticism and of the sweetness and sustenance of Christianity is communicated in these poems. If it is not, I alone am to blame and throw myself on the mercy of the Subject of that great poet of the Word on whose feast day this manuscript was completed.

Bonnie Bowman Thurston
The Anchorage, Wheeling, WV
Feast of St. John the Evangelist, 2013

About Paraclete Press

Who We Are

Paraclete Press is a publisher of books, recordings, and DVDs on Christian spirituality. Our publishing represents a full expression of Christian belief and practice—from Catholic to Evangelical, from Protestant to Orthodox.

We are the publishing arm of the Community of Jesus, an ecumenical monastic community in the Benedictine tradition. As such, we are uniquely positioned in the marketplace without connection to a large corporation and with informal relationships to many branches and denominations of faith.

What We Are Doing

Paraclete Press Books

Paraclete publishes books that show the richness and depth of what it means to be Christian. Although Benedictine spirituality is at the heart of all that we do, we publish books that reflect the Christian experience across many cultures, time periods, and houses of worship. We publish books that nourish the vibrant life of the church and its people—books about spiritual practice, formation, history, ideas, and customs.

We have several different series, including the best-selling Paraclete Essentials and Paraclete Giants series of classic texts in contemporary English; Voices from the Monastery—men and women monastics writing about living a spiritual life today; award-winning poetry; best-selling gift books for children on the occasions of baptism and first communion; and the Active Prayer Series that brings creativity and liveliness to any life of prayer.

Mount Tabor Books

Paraclete's Mount Tabor Books series focuses on liturgical worship, art and art history, ecumenism, and the first millennium church.

Paraclete Recordings

From Gregorian chant to contemporary American choral works, our music recordings celebrate sacred choral music through the centuries. Paraclete Recordings is the record label of the internationally acclaimed choir Gloriæ Dei Cantores, praised for their "rapt and fathomless spiritual intensity" by *American Record Guide,* and the Gloriæ Dei Cantores Schola, which specializes in the study and performance of Gregorian chant. Paraclete Press is also the exclusive North American distributor of the recordings of the Monastic Choir of St. Peter's Abbey in Solesmes, France, long considered to be a leading authority on Gregorian chant.

Paraclete Video Productions

Our DVDs offer spiritual help, healing, and biblical guidance for life issues: grief and loss, marriage, forgiveness, anger management, facing death, and spiritual formation.

LEARN MORE ABOUT US AT OUR WEBSITE

www.paracletepress.com

or phone us toll-free at 1.800.451.5006

SCAN TO READ MORE

Also available from PARACLETE POETRY

Unquiet Vigil
NEW AND SELECTED POEMS
BROTHER PAUL QUENON, OCSO

ISBN: 978-1-61261-560-8 | 176 pages
$21.99, French flap paperback

What might briefly tumble through a monk's mind, or be hard chiseled over a span of years; or what quietly emerges while sitting in the dark before dawn—these are the inner and outer landscapes of the poems found in *Unquiet Vigil* collected from five decades of living a monastic life.

Endless Life
POEMS OF THE MYSTICS
SCOTT CAIRNS

ISBN: 978-1-61261-520-2
160 pages
$18.00, Paperback

From Saint Paul to Julian of Norwich, Scott Cairns has lovingly examined, pressed for further revelation, and set in verse the most memorable, beautiful sayings of the fathers and mothers of Christianity.

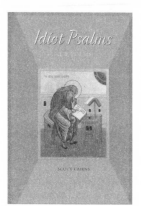

Idiot Psalms
NEW POEMS
SCOTT CAIRNS

ISBN: 978-1-61261-515-8
96 pages
$17.00, Paperback

A new collection from one of our favorite poets. Fourteen "Idiot Psalms," surrounded by dozens of other poems, make this his most challenging collection yet.